THE HANDY LITTLE GUIDE

Spiritual Communion

Our Sunday Visitor
Huntington, Indiana

Nihil Obstat
Msgr. Michael Heintz, Ph.D.
Censor Librorum

Imprimatur
✠ Kevin C. Rhoades
Bishop of Fort Wayne-South Bend

25 24 23 22 21 20 1 2 3 4 5 6 7 8 9

Our Sunday Visitor Publishing Division, Our Sunday Visitor, Inc., 200 Noll Plaza, Huntington, IN 46750; 1-800-348-2440; www.osv.com

ISBN: 978-1-68192-713-8 (Inventory No. T2587)
LCCN: 2020936097
1. RELIGION—Christian Living—Devotional.
2. RELIGION—Christian Rituals & Practice—General.
3. RELIGION—Christianity—Catholic.
eISBN: 978-1-68192-714-5

Printed in the United States

For Father Lloyd M. Bowden (1922–2019),
by whose ministry
I was reborn in the waters of baptism

Contents

Introduction

Catholics believe the holy Eucharist is the "source and summit" of our faith. When we receive holy Communion, we believe that we receive Jesus Christ himself, body, blood, soul, and divinity. Through the Eucharist we can be united to him in the closest way possible in this life. The innumerable gifts we receive in Communion draw us even more closely to Christ.

Yet sometimes we are not able to receive sacramental holy Communion.

At times this is because of our own actions or by our own choice. When we are in the state of mortal sin, by which we turn ourselves away from God, only sacramental confession can repair the relationship. Or perhaps the regulation to fast one hour prior to receiving Communion was not observed. Sometimes people choose to fast from Communion for the purposes of spiritual growth or out of a general sense of unworthiness.

Other times, we cannot receive holy Communion through no (or little) fault of our own. For instance, we might be restricted from access to the sacraments by sickness, handicap, or food allergy, or we might live in a remote area where sacraments are celebrated intermittently. Imprisonment, emergency travel, or other outstanding complications might also limit our access to the Eucharist. Finally, in dire circumstances, such as times of war or pestilence, Catholics could be prohibited from attending Mass and unable to receive Communion even outside of Mass unless as Viaticum (in danger of death).

Despite all of this, people of faith know that God does not abandon his people. Even when we cannot access the sacrament, God's grace is not closed off. As the *Catechism of the Catholic Church* reminds us, God "himself is not bound by his sacraments" (1257).

When situations prevent the reception of Communion, the Church offers remedies — one of which is making an act of *spiritual* communion.

Spiritual communion is a devotion for those who are unable, for whatever reason, to receive sacramental holy Communion. Any baptized Catholic can make an act of spiritual communion. There are no prescribed rituals; instead, this act of prayer has only two requirements: One must express belief in Christ's real presence in the Eucharist, and one must have a real desire for communion with him. (For more information on how to make an act of spiritual communion, see Acts of Spiritual Communion and Other Devotions, p. 62.)

What Makes Spiritual Communion Possible?

Before taking a look at the why and how of spiritual communion, we should ask: How is it possible? The practice of spiritual communion and our understanding of it depends on our understanding of the Church and the sacraments. Here we will take a look at the theological framework within which sacramental communion is situated.

Life in Christ

As creatures of the Almighty, we yearn for the living God. With the psalmist we can say, "As the deer longs for streams of water, so my soul longs for you, O God" (Ps 42:2). And with Saint Augustine (354–430) we can acknowledge, "You have made us for yourself, O Lord, and our heart is restless until it rests in you" (*Confessions* I.1).

The human soul longs for communion with God. This is possible through Jesus Christ, the Son of God made man, who died for our sins and rose from the dead. Through him we gain access to the divine life. Our very desire to seek communion with the Lord Jesus is rooted in the desire for divine life, which we access through him.

In fact, the greatest news available to us is that Jesus gives us life. Indeed, bestowing life on a people dead through sin was central to Christ's mission: "I came so that they might have life and have it more abundantly" (Jn 10:10). Death has no power over us thanks to what Jesus accomplished by his passion, death, resurrection, and ascension. His life is the prism through which we make sense of our own lives. Through the victory he won on Easter by rising from the dead, Christ opens up for us the way to eternal life.

As Christians, we know death no longer has power over us and heaven becomes our goal. At baptism we are ushered into the life of the Holy Trinity, the new life made accessible through Christ's sacrifice on the cross. God freely showers his grace upon us as we make our journey of faith, and he gives us this grace especially through the sacraments. The sacraments help conform us more closely to Christ and allow us to share in his life. Sharing in Christ's life means we are no longer enslaved by our sins, and God's forgiveness and mercy are made freely available to us. Not only that, our incorporation in the Church is accomplished, making us members of the Body of Christ. As Saint Paul tells us, "For in one Spirit we were all baptized into one body" (1 Cor 12:13).

One Body in Christ

The foundations for understanding the Church as the Body of Christ can be traced to her earliest days, notably in the pastoral letters and conversion experience of Saint Paul. When Saul, as he was known before his conversion, fell to the ground amid a blinding light, he realized, in hearing the voice of the Lord, that his persecution of Christians was really a persecution of Christ (see Acts 22:6–11).

Paul learned that Christ identifies as one with his followers. Together, believers in Christ form the Body of Christ, and this bond begun in baptism is fed, nourished, and reinforced through the Sacrament of the Eucharist. At baptism, and intensified through the Eucharist, Christ's believers are intimately grafted to him, forming what Saint Augustine described as the *totus Christus*, or the whole Christ, a body composed of Christ, our head, and us, his members. "I am the vine, you are the branches," Christ tells us. "Whoever remains in me and I in him will bear much fruit, because without me you can do nothing" (Jn 15:5).

The Eucharist is the usual way of intensifying this real and profound relationship with Christ. Yet there are times when reception of holy Communion is not possible. An act of spiritual communion can be a fitting means for us to acknowledge and give thanks for our communion with Christ made possible by our baptism. And it can keep alive for us the fruits of the Eucharist.

Christ himself tells us about the centrality of the Eucharist in the life of believers and its role in salvation: "Amen, amen, I say to you, unless you eat the flesh of the Son of Man and drink his blood, you do not have life within you. Whoever eats my flesh and drinks my blood has eternal life, and I will raise him on the last day. For my flesh is true food, and my blood is true drink" (Jn 6:53–55). In light of this revelation, we believe the Eucharist "preserves, increases, and renews the life of grace received at Baptism" (CCC 1392).

The Eucharist provides the foundation and nourishment for each disciple's transformation in Christ. "So whoever is in Christ is a new creation: the old things have passed away; behold, new things have come" (2 Cor 5:17). This transformation is a continual, lifelong process. Each day we take up the call to holiness and go about doing the work of Christ in the world. The Church, therefore, encourages regular reception of holy Communion to strengthen and sustain us.

Like baptism, we celebrate the Eucharist at the Lord's command: "Do this in memory of me." And yet, unlike baptism, which is never repeated, we celebrate the Eucharist again and again — indeed, "until he comes again."

Nonetheless, it is also important for us to understand the expectations of the Church regarding holy Communion. The Church's teaching on the matter is that Catholics are obliged to receive Communion only once a year (during the Easter season, often called our "Easter duty"), although we are obliged to attend Mass each Sunday and holy days of obligation (around sixty days or so each year). Daily reception of Communion is a more recent development in Catholic sacramental practice, especially encouraged as a spiritual good since the time of Pope Saint Pius X in the early twentieth century. Before that, many saints did not frequently receive holy Communion, such as Saint Louis IX (1214–70), the French monarch renowned for his sanctity, who received Communion only six times a year — and that was thought to be frequent at the time.

Living in Communion

Spiritual communion can allow us to participate in the inestimable fruits of receiving holy Communion.

Sacramental reception of holy Communion "augments our union with Christ" (CCC 1391). It "preserves, increases, and renews the life of grace received at Baptism," a life which "needs the nourishment of Eucharistic Communion" (1392). Through the graces made available from the Mass, all of God's people are able to conform themselves more closely to Christ and follow him.

Spiritual communion can open us up to these graces. It encourages us to pattern our behavior and activity on the activity of Christ alive in the Eucharist.

The practice of spiritual communion is

meant to connect us to the sacred realities present in the Eucharist when we are unable to sacramentally receive holy Communion. Even when we cannot receive Communion, we can live in communion with the Lord at all times.

Spiritual Worship

As our bond with Christ is intensified and augmented in holy Communion, we are given the grace to be more like him. Saint Paul also says our moral life, when properly ordered, is an act of worship. Worshiping God always and everywhere, we adopt a Eucharistic way of life, and we can worship at all times in living communion with Jesus. Paul says, "I urge you therefore, brothers, by the mercies of God, to offer your bodies as a living sacrifice, holy and pleasing to God, your spiritual worship" (Rom 12:1).

Here, as Pope Benedict XVI taught in his book *Called to Holiness*, Paul "speaks of the liturgy as life. We ourselves, our body; we in our body and as a body must be liturgy. …

The true liturgy is that of our body, of our being in the Body of Christ, just as Christ himself made the liturgy of the world, the cosmic liturgy, which strives to draw all people to itself."

"In brief," the *Catechism* states, "the Eucharist is the sum and summary of our faith: 'Our way of thinking is attuned to the Eucharist, and the Eucharist in turn confirms our way of thinking'"(1327). Therefore, certain aspects of the Eucharistic celebration can become characteristics of our lives, which can help us live in spiritual communion with the Lord and spiritually worship him at all times.

The Eucharist is primarily a celebration of gratitude. The Catechism teaches: "The Church expresses her gratitude to God for all his benefits, for all that he has accomplished through creation, redemption, and sanctification. Eucharist means first of all 'thanksgiving'" (1360). Cardinal Francis E. George, O.M.I., explained this centrality of gratitude: "Gratitude to God shapes our lives, at their beginning and their end. Each moment is a gift; each event unfolds under God's loving Providence." Living in communion with Christ, living eucharistically, we give thanks for everything, knowing with Saint Paul "that all things work for good for those who love God" (Rom 8:28).

The consecration is the heart of each Mass, where Christ's sacrifice on the cross is perpetuated in every time and place. The *Catechism* explains: "The lives of the faithful, their praise, sufferings, prayer, and work, are united with those of Christ and with his total offering, and so acquire a new value. Christ's sacrifice present on the altar makes it possible for all generations of Christians to be united with his offering" (1368). Present or not, all Christians are united to this sacrifice, since the Mass is the work of all God's people. We consecrate our lives to Christ and can grow in communion with him, day in and day out, moment by moment, when we unite our lives to his sacrifice of praise.

Growth in Charity

Another name for the Eucharist is the "Sacred Liturgy," which illustrates how it binds us together in our common identity and purpose. The word "liturgy" itself is rooted in a phrase meaning work of, or on behalf of, the people. The liturgy is the participation of God's people in his work. "In the New Testament the word 'liturgy' refers not only to the celebration of divine worship but also to the proclamation of the Gospel and to active charity" (CCC 1070).

In his encyclical *Deus Caritas Est*, Pope Benedict XVI wrote:

> Union with Christ is also union with all those to whom he gives himself. I cannot possess Christ just for myself; I can belong to him only in union with all those who have become, or who will become, his own. Communion draws me out of myself towards him, and thus also towards unity with all Christians.

> We become "one body," completely joined in a single existence. Love of God and love of neighbor are now truly united: God incarnate draws us all to himself. (14)

Holy Communion fortifies us against sin and intensifies our charity. Receiving Christ's body makes present within us the redemption and salvation won for us. Saint Ambrose (d. 397) taught, recounted in the *Catechism*: "For as often as we eat this bread and drink the cup, we proclaim the death of the Lord. If we proclaim the Lord's death, we proclaim the forgiveness of sins. If, as often as his blood is poured out, it is poured for the forgiveness of sins, I should always receive it, so that it may always forgive my sins. Because I always sin, I should always have a remedy" (1393).

Saint Augustine explains that our "Amen" at the time of holy Communion is our way of acknowledging our identity in Christ. We can say that same "Amen" by our lives, through our spiritual worship and spiritual communion with Christ. "You are saying 'Amen' to what you are: your response is a personal signature, affirming your faith. … Be a member of Christ's body, then, so that your 'Amen' may ring true!" (Sermon 272).

Communion When You Can't Receive Communion

Saint Teresa of Avila (1515–82), in *The Way of Perfection*, wrote: "When you do not receive communion and you do not attend Mass, you can make a spiritual communion, which is a most beneficial practice; by it the love of God will be greatly impressed on you." Making an act of spiritual communion allows us to express our heart's longing for the Lord and our belief in his Eucharistic presence, even when we are unable to receive holy Communion.

As mentioned in the introduction, there are many circumstances under which we may not be able to receive Communion.

Catholics are obliged to refrain from reception of holy Communion when in the state of mortal sin. Paul invites us to an examination of conscience before receiving Communion: "Therefore whoever eats the bread or drinks the cup of the Lord unworthily will have to answer for the body and blood of the Lord. A person should examine himself, and so eat the bread and drink the cup. For anyone who eats and drinks without discerning the body, eats and drinks judgment on himself" (1 Cor 11:27–29).

Although the Church encourages frequent reception of Communion, we must be in the state of grace. This means, at a minimum, that we cannot receive the Eucharist when we are in the state of mortal sin. This is because such sin cuts us off from God and fractures our relationship with him. God's mercy and forgiveness are showered upon us in the Sacrament of Reconciliation, which heals and restores us to proper relationship with God. If confession is not available, it might be appropriate in such situations to make an act of spiritual communion, which can help us recognize our desire to live in unity with the Lord and is a means to fortify us in the struggle against sin.

Catholics also are obliged to refrain from food or drink (other than water) for an hour before reception of Communion. Not observing this fast would ordinarily leave one unable to receive Communion. (However, there can be various reasons that might provide for a dispensation from this obligation, and these can be sought in consultation with a pastor.) If you have not been able to keep the Eucharistic fast, an act of spiritual communion is appropriate.

Many other reasons might prevent someone from attending Mass or receiving Communion, which are opportunities in which spiritual communion can be beneficial to the soul.

Consider the homebound or the hospitalized who are unable to receive the Eucharist as frequently as they would like. Or we might be sick and therefore unable to attend Mass. In times like these, we can depend on the prayers of others and unite ourselves fervently to the Church's prayer. A spiritual communion can be a brief, simple way of uniting ourselves to the prayers of the Church and expressing the desire for union with the Lord through the Church.

Some Catholics live in distant regions without frequent access to the sacraments. This is becoming more common even in certain regions of the United States today due to a shortage of priests. In other parts of the world, such as in certain places in Africa or the Amazon region of South America, reception of holy Communion is a treasured rarity for the faithful.

Or there are immigrants and refugees, imprisoned Catholics, or those who are suffering the effects of war, disaster, or an outbreak of infectious disease. Such situations might make it impossible for Catholics to attend Mass or even to receive Communion outside of Mass, except in cases of approaching death.

It is important to remember, especially for those unable to receive holy Communion through no fault of their own, that God is always active and at work in our lives. Although he established the sacraments as the ordinary means to give us his grace, God is not bound by his sacraments (see CCC 1257). In the end, God does not expect the impossible, nor does he hold such circumstances against us.

In those circumstances, Catholics are not deprived of the graces and fruits of the Eucharist. On the contrary, the Council of Trent taught that those who receive communion spiritually "experience its fruit and benefit from it." Echoing that, a 1983 letter from the Holy See's Congregation for the Doctrine of the Faith stated:

> Individual faithful or communities who because of persecution or lack of priests are deprived of the holy Eucharist for either a short or longer period of time, do not thereby

> lack the grace of the Redeemer. If they are intimately animated by a desire for the sacrament and united in prayer with the whole Church, and call upon the Lord and raise their hearts to him, by virtue of the Holy Spirit they live in communion with the whole Church, the living body of Christ, and with the Lord himself. Through their desire for the sacrament in union with the Church, no matter how distant they may be physically, they are intimately and really united to her and therefore receive the fruits of the sacrament.

One small note: Some attention to language is important. "Communion" expresses the communal nature of our faith, it is not "co-union," — just "me and Jesus." This is because when we receive the Eucharist, or make an act of spiritual communion, we enter into communion with Christ *and* the members of his body, the Church. In communion with the Church, then, we submit ourselves to the Church's tradition and authority. Because the sacraments are gifts from Christ, not rights, we receive them on his terms — which are the Church's terms — and never on our own terms. Such a perspective can be helpful when considering the times in which we might be unable to receive holy Communion for one reason or another.

Spiritual Communion for Spiritual Growth

Acts of spiritual communion can increase our desire to achieve fuller unity with Christ in holy Communion. The more we express our longing to receive the Eucharist, the more likely we are to make it a priority. There is grace even in expressing our desire for Christ in the Eucharist, which can be an impetus to help us reorganize and reprioritize our spiritual lives.

Sometimes life gets unwieldy and we cannot pray as often or as much as we might like. There are times we might like to attend a weekday Mass but are precluded by work, domestic duties, or a score of other legitimate obligations. Or we might want to commit to prayer before the Blessed Sacrament yet somehow cannot find the time. Or we may find ourselves in periods of spiritual dryness, which deeper hunger for Christ can help rectify.

Acts of spiritual communion can increase our desire to achieve fuller unity with Christ in holy Communion. The more we express our longing to receive the Eucharist, the more apt we might be to make it a priority. There is grace even in expressing our desire for Christ in the Eucharist, which can be an impetus to help us reorganize and reprioritize our spiritual lives.

There is also the practice of refraining from the Eucharist for the purposes of spiritual growth. By adopting a fast from the Eucharist, one can intensify one's appreciation for the Sacrament. As the saying goes, "absence makes the heart grow fonder." This is a spiritual program in which one willingly adopts spiritual communion for a given time, which has been considered spiritually beneficial throughout the Church's tradition. Considering this possibility can be consoling at times when it is impossible to receive holy Communion, to help us know even in such circumstances we can grow in our spiritual lives.

"Do we not often take the reception of the Blessed Sacrament too lightly?" Pope Benedict XVI pondered. "Might not this kind of spiritual fasting be of service, or even necessary, to deepen and renew our relationship to the Body of Christ?"

He suggested such Eucharistic fasting "could lead to a deepening of personal relationship with the Lord in the sacrament. It could also be an act of solidarity with all those who yearn for the sacrament but cannot receive it. ... Sometimes we need hunger, physical and spiritual hunger, if we are to come fresh to the Lord's gifts and understand the suffering of our hungering brothers. Both spiritual and physical hunger can be a vehicle of love" (*Behold the Pierced One*, Ignatius Press, 1986)

Nevertheless, the *Catechism* teaches that "the Church warmly recommends that the faithful receive Holy Communion when they participate in the celebration of the Eucharist" (1417).

A Traditional Practice

The practice of spiritual communion has been taught and recommended throughout the Church's tradition by countless pastors and saints. Spiritual communion was a daily practice for many saints, even if they attended daily Mass. It is said that Saint Francis de Sales (1567–1622) made a practice of reciting an act of spiritual communion on the quarters of each hour so that he might connect all things to Christ's action made present in the Eucharist.

Saint Catherine of Siena (1347–80) had a vision of the Lord in which he told her about the value of spiritual communion. She believed that a spiritual communion was without value since it did not come close to sacramental communion. So Jesus showed her two ciboriums and said, "In this golden ciborium I put your sacramental Communions. In this silver ciborium I put your spiritual Communions. Both ciboriums are quite pleasing to me."

Undying Hunger

Some of the saints found spiritual communion to be a means to satisfy, at least temporarily, their intense hunger for communion with the Lord throughout the day.

Saint Pio of Pietrelcina (1887–1968) once wrote of how he longed for communion with Christ from the earliest moments of his day, and how even the Eucharist did not suffice for his longing for total unity with him. "I have such a thirst and hunger before receiving Him that it's a wonder I don't die of anxiety." And even after receiving him in holy Communion at Mass, he wrote:

> My thirst and hunger do not diminish after I have received Him in the Blessed Sacrament, but rather, increase steadily. Oh, how sweet

> was the conversation I held with Paradise this morning. The heart of Jesus and my own, if you will pardon the expression, fused. They were no longer two hearts beating but only one. My heart disappeared as if it were a drop in the ocean.

Saint Thérèse of Lisieux (1873–97) experienced something similar in her spiritual life. Even though a daily communicant in her Carmelite monastery, the Little Flower had an undying hunger for union with the Eucharistic Lord, expressed clearly in a poem, "Desires near the Tabernacle." She wrote:

> I would like to be the chalice there, where I would adore the Divine Blood. I can however in the Holy Sacrifice, gather it in me every morning. My soul is therefore more dear to Jesus, it is more precious than vessels of gold.

Other saints were forced to refrain from holy Communion as punishment or as a test for spiritual growth. In times when we are unable to receive Communion, we can turn to their example and grow in longing for the Eucharist by making our own their great love and desire for the sacrament.

When in jail for several years, mistakenly believed to be a danger to society, Saint Rocco (1295–1327) spent his time looking out the window of a jail cell. A guard once asked what he was always staring at. "I am looking at the tower of the parish church," he replied. He knew where Christ was, and he joined himself to Christ in his heart.

Once, as a test, a confessor instructed Saint Gemma Galgani (1878–1903) not to receive holy Communion. Writing to explain the situation to her spiritual director, she said, "O my Father, my pen does not want to write more, my hand shakes strongly, I cry."

Saint Gerard Majella (1726–55) refused to defend himself when he was once falsely accused of misconduct. As punishment, he was deprived of the Eucharist. His longing to receive the Eucharistic Lord was so strong that he one day refused to serve the Mass, explaining, "on seeing Jesus in the Host in the hands of the priest, I would not be able to resist taking by force the Host from his hands."

Pastoral Wisdom

Many saintly shepherds exhorted those in their charge to make spiritual communion a daily practice.

Saint Jean-Marie Vianney (1786–1859), recommended the practice of spiritual communion as a way to avoid taking the sacrament for granted:

> If we are deprived of Sacramental Communion, let us replace it, as far as we can, by spiritual communion, which we can make every moment; for we ought to have always a burning desire to receive the good God.

> ... After the reception of the Sacraments, when we feel ourselves slacken in the love of God, let us have recourse at once to spiritual communion. When we cannot come to the church, let us turn towards the tabernacle; no wall can shut us out from the good God.

Saint Josemaría Escrivá (1902–75) encouraged a spiritual communion at least once daily as a way to make amends for sacrileges against the Eucharist:

> Do not neglect to say, "Jesus, I love you," and make one spiritual communion, at least, each day, in atonement for all the profanations and sacrileges he suffers because he wants to be with us.

In his 2003 encyclical letter *Ecclesia de Eucharistia*, Pope Saint John Paul II recommended the practice of spiritual communion for the good effects it can have in our spiritual lives:

> The Eucharist thus appears as the culmination of all the sacraments in perfecting our communion with God the Father by identification with his only-begotten Son through the working of the Holy Spirit. With discerning faith a distinguished writer of the Byzantine tradition voiced this truth: in the Eucharist "unlike any other sacrament, the mystery [of communion] is so perfect that it brings us to the heights of every good thing: here is the ultimate goal of every human desire, because here we attain God and God joins himself to us in the most perfect union." Precisely for this reason it is good to cultivate in our hearts a constant desire for the sacrament of the Eucharist. This was the origin of the practice

of "spiritual communion," which has happily been established in the Church for centuries and recommended by saints who were masters of the spiritual life. (34)

When We Cannot Attend Mass

There are times when attendance at Mass and reception of holy Communion might not be possible. Situations that make Mass impossible might include emergency travel, illness (of yourself or a loved one), times of war, crisis, or risk of infectious disease. During these times, we can use a variety of other means to deepen our relationship with the Lord.

Although we might long for fuller unity and communion with the Lord, we can find consolation in his own words: "For where two or three are gathered together in my name, there am I in the midst of them" (Mt 18:20). Christ promised, "I am with you always, until the end of the age" (Mt 28:20).

As Cardinal Francis George, O.M.I. summarized this reality: "The risen Lord will never abandon his people. Those who find their personal identity in relation to him will never be alone."

It is also comforting to remember that each and every Mass is an act of the whole People of God. Regardless of who is present, Mass is offered to the Lord, by the priest, on behalf of all God's people and in the name of Christ. Renewing the gift of our baptism, the Mass makes present again and again the means to participate in Christ's action: his passion, death, resurrection, and ascension. By those mysteries, we obtain the lens through which we make sense of the world. Christ's sacrifice stands at the center of human salvation, and the Eucharist is the means he provided for us to participate in it. Even when we cannot receive Christ sacramentally, we can unite ourselves with his sacrifice spiritually.

Here are some recommended practices for those times when Mass and the Eucharist are not available to you:

- Gather together in small communities, at least those with whom you live. You might choose to observe a liturgical service of the Word, using the Introductory Rites of the Mass and the readings from the Lectionary, and concluding with an act of spiritual communion.
- Unite yourself with the Lord through reading, studying, praying with, and discussing the Scriptures. Make use of the daily readings offered in the Lectionary, which are widely available on the internet or through mobile apps.
- Practice *lectio divina*, a meditative, reflective method of praying with the Word of God.

(For more information see chapter 6)

- Encounter the Lord through the psalms and prayers of the Liturgy of the Hours, which, the *Catechism* states, "is like an extension of the Eucharistic celebration, does not exclude but rather in a complementary way calls forth the various devotions of the People of God, especially adoration and worship of the Blessed Sacrament" (1178).

- Pray the Rosary, which, Saint John Paul noted, puts us "in living communion with Jesus" (*Rosarium Virginis Mariae*, No. 2).

- Participate in Masses aired on television or livestreamed over the internet.

- Sit down with a spiritual classic or the biography of a saint and find Christ active and alive.

- Reflect on one of the Eucharistic prayers from the Mass or a Eucharistic hymn, such as *Pange Lingua* or *O Salutaris Hostia*.

Any and all of these efforts, while in no way a replacement for the Mass or reception of holy Communion, can mystically unite us to the Church's prayer, especially the Masses celebrated around the world on our behalf. These practices also unite us more closely with Christ by deepening the relationship with him that began at our baptism.

Communion with Christ through Scripture

"The Church has always venerated the Scriptures as she venerates the Lord's Body. She never ceases to present to the faithful the bread of life, taken from the one table of God's Word and Christ's Body" (CCC 103).

We grow in union with the Lord through reading the Scriptures; indeed, Christ feeds us with his word, which the Second Vatican Council's Dogmatic Constitution on Divine Revelation (*Dei Verbum*) calls "food for the soul."

"The Church has always venerated the divine Scriptures just as she venerates the body of the Lord, since, especially in the sacred liturgy, she unceasingly receives and offers to the faithful the bread of life from the table both of God's word and of Christ's body" (*DV* 21). And so, even if we are unable to attend Mass or receive holy Communion, we can unite ourselves with the Lord through reading, studying, praying with, and discussing the Scriptures.

As for the disciples on the road to Emmaus, the Word of God gestures toward the Eucharist. When we are nourished by Scripture, we are drawn more closely to Christ: "Were not our hearts burning [within us] while he spoke to us on the way and opened the scriptures to us?" (Lk 24:32) those disciples said of their encounter with the Lord on Easter morning. Indeed, the Lord "was made known to them in the breaking of the bread" (Lk 24:35).

Lectio divina is a popular method of meditating on Scripture. It gives us an opportunity to intensify our relationship with Christ. This explanation from Cardinal George will be sure to assist anyone who uses it to enter a deeper communion with the Lord:

> First of all, every prayer is through Christ our Lord, "through him, with him and in him," as the Eucharistic prayer concludes. The source of every prayer is therefore an encounter with Christ, a union with him in mind and heart. Since Holy Scripture is the written witness to Christ, praying with Sacred Scripture is a privileged way to come to know him surely and to love him devotedly. At the beginning of our prayer with Scripture, we should ask the Holy Spirit, sent upon the Church by the Risen Christ, to guide our prayer.
>
> Reading: What does the Word of God mean in itself? The first step in praying with Scripture is to read the text slowly and thoughtfully, perhaps aloud. A contemporary biblical commentary that helps us to understand the context of the hu-

man author is useful for shedding light on hard passages. Who are the principle personages in the selected passage? Is there a use of images or symbols? What is the controlling message that the human writer meant to convey? A commentary by a spiritual author recognized by the Church can also help uncover meanings that the divine author meant to teach through the inspired text.

Meditation: What does the Word of God mean for me? The second step in praying with Scripture is to ask what God might be telling me personally as I read. What is important to me about this text? Why? Is there a call to me in what I read? With what personage in the text do I identify? How am I being asked to change? If we try to identify personally with the biblical text we are reading, light might be shed and reflections might come to mind that are new to us. These are graces given to us to see our lives anew in the light of God's word.

Prayer: What desires does the Word of God place in my heart? In the midst of the prayerful reading of Holy Scripture, we should find ourselves wanting to ask something of God. We have listened to God's word and meditated upon it. What does it move us to ask for? What do we say in response to the Word of God? Gratitude is one response, but prayer might also move us to simplify our lives and to act in a way consistent with God's word to us. We often do not leave the time of prayer with specific plans in mind; but we should always leave with more courage to face the demands of life in the light of God's word.

Contemplation: How does the Word of God shape us? Sometimes at the end of our reading, meditation, and prayer, God takes over our spiritual life and gives us a moment of special unity with him. These fruits of the spiritual reading of Sacred Scripture come seldom or often, depending upon the person. Always, they are meant to increase our intimacy with God and prepare us for loving him forever. In Holy Scripture, God is the principal author and actor. In contemplative prayer, God "writes" our lives so that Christ lives in us.

The steps outlined above are not a rigid schema. They are helps to organize the time spent praying with Sacred Scripture; but the most important element of prayer is simply taking time. (Cardinal Francis E. George, O.M.I., first appeared in *The Catholic New World*, November 9, 2008)

Acts of Spiritual Communion and Other Devotions

While there is no set formula or rite to make an act of spiritual communion, there are certain expectations.

Before making an act of spiritual communion, we need to seek the Lord's pardon and forgiveness for sins.[1] It is customary to include some sort of penitential act and make an Act of Contrition, like one of the following:

I confess to almighty God, and to you, my

1. As always, if in the state of mortal sin, we should plan to make a sacramental confession as soon as possible. If unable to receive sacramental Communion at a particular time, we can still make an act of spiritual communion and express contrition for our sins.

brothers and sisters, that I have greatly sinned, in my thoughts and in my words, in what I have done and in what I have failed to do, through my fault, through my fault, through my most grievous fault; therefore I ask blessed Mary ever-Virgin, all the Angels and Saints, and you, my brothers and sisters, to pray for me to the Lord our God. Amen.

My God, I am sorry for my sins with all my heart. In choosing to do wrong and failing to do good, I have sinned against you whom I should love above all things. I firmly intend, with your help, to do penance, to sin no more, and to avoid whatever leads me to sin. Our savior Jesus Christ, suffered and died for us. In his name, my God, have mercy. Amen.

To make an act of spiritual communion, it is important to meet three criteria:

1. We must express our faith, particularly belief in the real presence of Christ in the Eucharist.

2. We must express our desire to be united sacramentally with Christ in the Eucharist.
3. We must express our desire to stay united with Christ and enjoy the fruits made available through sacramental reception of holy Communion.

These fundamental aspects are included in a variety of prayers that have become part of the tradition for use when making an act of spiritual communion. Included below are a selection of these prayers.

ACTS OF SPIRITUAL COMMUNION

An Act of Spiritual Communion by Saint Alphonsus Liguori

My Jesus, I believe that you are present in the most Blessed Sacrament. I love you above all things and I desire to receive you into my soul. Since I cannot now receive you sacramentally, come at least spiritually into my heart. I embrace you as if you were already there, and unite myself wholly to you. Never permit me to be separated from you. Amen.

An Act of Spiritual Communion

O Jesus! you hast given us in the holy Eucharist your Body and Blood to be our spiritual nourishment, through which we may have life everlasting. Would that I were now prepared to approach the Holy Table to be united with you in the Blessed Sacrament! I desire, with all my heart, to receive this living Bread which came down from heaven.

O Lord, I am not worthy that you should
enter under my roof;
but only say the word, and my soul shall
be healed.
O Lord, I am not worthy that you should
enter under my roof;
but only say the word, and my soul shall
be healed.
O Lord, I am not worthy that you should
enter under my roof;
but only say the word, and my soul shall
be healed.

Let me taste, at least, the sweetness of a spiritual communion. Come to me, Jesus, my Lord, my Master. Come and refresh my soul. Strengthen me, that in union with you I may do perfectly the heavenly Father's will. Let me never be separated from you by sin. Keep me in your love and your grace. I will not be lured away from you by the deceitful honors and pleasures of the world. I love you above all things and with my whole heart. You are the God of my heart, and the God that is my portion forever. Increase my faith, strengthen my hope, kindle my love, that I may die to self and live but for you.

An Act of Spiritual Communion with Mary

Mother of the Redeemer, Mary full of grace, with you I honor and worship your Son, Jesus Christ, present to us under the form of bread and wine. I believe he is really and truly present to us in the Eucharist as he was nursing from your breast near the manger at Bethlehem or lying in your arms at the foot of the cross at Calvary.

With you, I love him and adore him with unshakable faith in his love for us. Unable to receive him now in sacramental Communion, I beg that he come dwell in my heart, as he came to dwell in your womb after giving your consent to Gabriel. Lord Jesus, hasten to come and abide in me and never let me be parted from you. Amen.

An Act of Spiritual Communion with St. Joseph

Glorious St. Joseph, guardian of Our Lord and spouse of Mary, come to my aid. Pray that Jesus will come to me just as he chose to dwell under your fatherly care. I firmly believe that he is present in the Eucharist, body, blood, soul and divinity — just as present still as he was in your arms after his holy birth at Bethlehem. Although I cannot receive him now in sacramental Communion, beg him to reside in my heart just as he did at your home in Nazareth. Lord Jesus, hasten to come and abide in me and never let me be parted from you. Amen.

OTHER PRAYERS

Anima Christi

Soul of Christ, be my sanctification;
Body of Christ, be my salvation;
Blood of Christ, fill all my veins;
Water of Christ's side, wash out my stains;
Passion of Christ, my comfort be;
O good Jesus, listen to me;
In thy wounds I fain would hide;
Ne'er to be parted from thy side;
Guard me, should the foe assail me;
Call me when my life shall fail me;
Bid me come to thee above,
With thy saints to sing thy love,
World without end. Amen.

(attributed to Pope John XXII and translated by Saint John Henry Newman)

O Jesus, Living in Mary

O Jesus, living in Mary, come and live in your servants:
in the spirit of your holiness,
in the fullness of your power,
in the reality of your virtues.
in the perfection of your ways,
in the communion of your mysteries;
have dominion over every adverse power,
in your own Spirit, to the glory of the Father.
Amen.

The Divine Praises

Blessed be God.

Blessed be his Holy Name.

Blessed be Jesus Christ, true God and true Man.

Blessed be the Name of Jesus.

Blessed be his most Sacred Heart.

Blessed be his most Precious Blood.

Blessed be Jesus in the most Holy Sacrament of the Altar.

Blessed be the Holy Spirit, the Paraclete.

Blessed be the great Mother of God, Mary most holy.

Blessed be her holy and Immaculate Conception.

Blessed be her glorious Assumption.

Blessed be the name of Mary, Virgin and Mother.

Blessed be St. Joseph, her most chaste spouse.

Blessed be God in his angels and in his saints.

May the heart of Jesus, in the Most Blessed Sacrament, be praised, adored, and loved with grateful affection, at every moment, in all the tabernacles of the world, even to the end of time. Amen.

Litany of the Holy Eucharist

Lord, have mercy on us.
Christ, have mercy on us.

Lord, have mercy on us. Christ, hear us.
Christ, graciously hear us.

God the Father of Heaven,
Have mercy on us.

God the Son, Redeemer of the world,
Have mercy on us.

God the Holy Spirit,
Have mercy on us.

Holy Trinity, One God,
Have mercy on us.

Jesus, living Bread which came down from heaven,
Have mercy on us.

Jesus, Bread from Heaven giving life to the

world,
Have mercy on us.

Jesus, hidden God and Savior,
Have mercy on us.

Jesus, who has loved us with an everlasting love,
Have mercy on us.

Jesus, whose delights are to be with the children of men,
Have mercy on us.

Jesus, who has given your Flesh for the life of the world,
Have mercy on us.

Jesus, who invites all to come to you,
Have mercy on us.

Jesus, who promises eternal life to those who receive you,
Have mercy on us.

Jesus, who with desire desires to eat this
Pasch with us,
Have mercy on us.

Jesus, ever ready to receive and welcome us,
Have mercy on us.

Jesus, who stands at our door knocking,
Have mercy on us.

Jesus, who has said that if we will open to you
the door,
you wilt come in and sup with us,
Have mercy on us.

Jesus, who receives us into your arms
and blesses us with the little children,
Have mercy on us.

Jesus, who suffers us to sit at your feet with
Magdalen,
Have mercy on us.

Jesus, who invites us to lean on your bosom

with the beloved disciple,
Have mercy on us.

Jesus, who has not left us orphans,
Have mercy on us.

Most dear Sacrament,
Have mercy on us.

Sacrament of love,
Have mercy on us.

Sacrament of sweetness,
Have mercy on us.
Life-giving Sacrament,
Have mercy on us.

Sacrament of strength,
Have mercy on us.

My God and my all,
Have mercy on us.

That our hearts may pant after you

as the heart after the fountains of water,
we beg you, hear us.

That you would manifest yourself to us
as to the two disciples in the breaking of bread,
we beg you, hear us.

That we may know your voice like Magdalen,
we beg you, hear us.

That with a lively faith we may confess
with the beloved disciple, "It is the Lord,"
we beg you, hear us.

That you would bless us who have not seen and yet have believed,
we beg you, hear us.

That we may love you in the Blessed Sacrament
with our whole heart, with our whole soul,
with all our mind, and with all our strength,

we beg you, hear us.

That the fruit of each Communion may be fresh love,
we beg you, hear us.

That our one desire may be to love you and to do your will,
we beg you, hear us.
That we may ever remain in your love,
we beg you, hear us.

That you would teach us how to receive and welcome you,
we beg you, hear us.

That you would teach us to pray, and yourself pray within us,
we beg you, hear us.

That with you every virtue may come into our souls,
we beg you, hear us.

That throughout this day you would keep us
closely united to you,
we beg you, hear us.

That you would give us grace to persevere to
the end,
we beg you, hear us.

That you would then be our support and Viaticum,
we beg you, hear us.

That with you and leaning on you
we may safely pass through all dangers,
we beg you, hear us.

That our last act may be one of perfect love
and our last breath a long deep sigh
to be in Our Father's house,
we beg you, hear us.

That your sweet face may smile upon us
when we appear before you,
we beg you, hear us.

That our banishment from you,
dearest Lord, may not be very long,
we beg you, hear us.

That when the time is come,
we may fly up from our prison to you,
and in your Sacred Heart find our rest forever,
we beg you, hear us.

Lamb of God, who takest away the sins of the world,
Spare us, O Lord.

Lamb of God, who takest away the sins of the world,
Graciously hear us, O Lord.

Lamb of God, who takest away the sins of the world,
Have mercy on us.

V. Stay with us, Lord, because it is toward evening,
R. And the day is now far spent.

Let Us Pray

We come to you, dear Lord, with the apostles, saying, "Increase our faith." Give us a strong and lively faith in the mystery of your Real Presence in the midst of us. Give us the splendid faith of the centurion, which drew from you such praise. Give us the faith of the beloved disciple to know you in the dark and say, "It is the Lord!" Give us the faith of Martha to confess, "You are the Christ, the Son of the living God." Give us the faith of Magdalen to fall at your feet crying, "Rabboni, Master." Give us the faith of all your saints, to whom the Blessed Sacrament has been heaven begun on earth. In every Communion increase our faith, our love, our humility, and our reverence, and all good will come into our souls. Dearest Lord, increase our faith. Amen.

About the Author

Michael R. Heinlein is editor of Our Sunday Visitor's Simply Catholic and a frequent contributor to many OSV publications. A graduate of The Catholic University of America, his service to the Church has also included parish ministry and teaching. He lives in Indiana with his wife and two children.